GW00731270

this journal belongs to:

_____

tips before you begin

1. Get clear on positive focus. Always focus on what you do want, not what you don't want. Remember: Whatever you focus on expands.

2. Work with the same intention for a set amount of time until you achieve it. Multiple intentions are difficult to achieve all at once for beginners.

3. In order to achieve your desires you must act on them. Look out for signs and cues and act on these. Feeling inspired? Do it!

4. Your feelings help you to understand your thoughts. If you are feeling happy, you will have happy thoughts.

5. Give often and be kind always. The more you give, the more you shall receive.

6. Have fun with your visualisations. You can have anything you want.

7. Have unwavering faith that the Universe has heard your request and is actively moving everything in your life to manifest your desires.

8. Expect miracles but do not become desperate.

Short term goals

Long term goals

Notes

Appreciation list

Dates to remember

Jan

Feb

Mar

Apr

May

Jun

Jul

Aug

Sep

Oct

Nov

Dec

"thoughts become things- if you can see it in your mind, you will hold it in your hand."

-Bob Proctor

Morning Meditation

Date: / /

todays focus:

_____

_____

_____

Affirmations for today:

_____

_____

_____

_____

Sleep I had last night:

Self-care to do today:

Things I am grateful for today:

_____

_____

_____

_____

_____

Evening Reflection

Date: / /

Positive thoughts and feelings about today:

_____

_____

_____

Positive things that happened today:

_____

_____

_____

_____

How I felt today:

Happy	Inspired
Motivated	Optimistic
Creative	Excited
Focused	Hopeful
Reflective	

A goal for tomorrow:

Morning Meditation

Date: / /

todays focus:

_____
_____
_____

Affirmations for today:

_____
_____
_____
_____

Sleep I had last night:

Self-care to do today:

Things I am grateful for today:

_____
_____
_____
_____
_____

Evening Reflection

Date: / /

Positive thoughts and feelings about today:

Positive things that happened today:

How I felt today:

Happy	Inspired
Motivated	Optimistic
Creative	Excited
Focused	Hopeful
Reflective	

A goal for tomorrow:

Morning Meditation

Date: /   /

todays focus:

Affirmations for today:

Sleep I had last night:

Self-care to do today:

things I am grateful for today:

Evening Reflection

Date: / /

Positive thoughts and feelings about today:

_____

_____

_____

_____

Positive things that happened today:

_____

_____

_____

_____

_____

How I felt today:

Happy	Inspired
Motivated	Optimistic
Creative	Excited
Focused	Hopeful
Reflective	

A goal for tomorrow:

Morning Meditation

Date: / /

todays focus:

_____
_____
_____

Affirmations for today:

_____
_____
_____
_____

Sleep I had last night:

Self-care to do today:

things I am grateful for today:

_____
_____
_____
_____
_____

Evening Reflection

Date: / /

Positive thoughts and feelings about today:

Positive things that happened today:

How I felt today:

Happy	Inspired
Motivated	Optimistic
Creative	Excited
Focused	Hopeful
Reflective	

A goal for tomorrow:

Morning Meditation

Date: /   /

todays focus:

_____
_____
_____

Affirmations for today:

_____
_____
_____
_____

Sleep I had last night:

Self-care to do today:

Things I am grateful for today:

_____
_____
_____
_____
_____

Evening Reflection

Date: / /

Positive thoughts and feelings about today:

_____
_____
_____
_____

Positive things that happened today:

_____
_____
_____
_____
_____

How I felt today:

Happy	Inspired
Motivated	Optimistic
Creative	Excited
Focused	Hopeful
Reflective	

A goal for tomorrow:

"Every time you feel good about something you are telling the Universe, 'More of this, please.'"

-Abraham Hicks

Morning Meditation

Date: / /

todays focus:

_____
_____
_____

Affirmations for today:

_____
_____
_____
_____

Sleep I had last night:

Self-care to do today:

things I am grateful for today:

_____
_____
_____
_____
_____

Evening Reflection

Date: / /

Positive thoughts and feelings about today:

_____

_____

_____

_____

Positive things that happened today:

_____

_____

_____

_____

_____

How I felt today:

Happy	Inspired
Motivated	Optimistic
Creative	Excited
Focused	Hopeful
Reflective	

A goal for tomorrow:

Morning Meditation

Date: / /

todays focus:

_____

_____

_____

Affirmations for today:

_____

_____

_____

_____

Sleep I had last night:

Self-care to do today:

things I am grateful for today:

_____

_____

_____

_____

_____

Evening Reflection

Date: / /

Positive thoughts and feelings about today:

Positive things that happened today:

How I felt today:

Happy	Inspired
Motivated	Optimistic
Creative	Excited
Focused	Hopeful
Reflective	

A goal for tomorrow:

Morning Meditation

Date: / /

todays focus:

Affirmations for today:

Sleep I had last night:

Self-care to do today:

things I am grateful for today:

Evening Reflection

Date: / /

Positive thoughts and feelings about today:

Positive things that happened today:

How I felt today:

Happy	Inspired
Motivated	Optimistic
Creative	Excited
Focused	Hopeful
Reflective	

A goal for tomorrow:

Morning Meditation

Date: /   /

todays focus:

Affirmations for today:

Sleep I had last night:

Self-care to do today:

things I am grateful for today:

Evening Reflection

Date: / /

Positive thoughts and feelings about today:

_____

_____

_____

_____

Positive things that happened today:

_____

_____

_____

_____

How I felt today:

Happy	Inspired
Motivated	Optimistic
Creative	Excited
Focused	Hopeful
Reflective	

A goal for tomorrow:

Morning Meditation

Date: / /

todays focus:

_____

_____

_____

Affirmations for today:

_____

_____

_____

_____

Sleep I had last night:

Self-care to do today:

things I am grateful for today:

_____

_____

_____

_____

_____

Evening Reflection

Date: / /

Positive thoughts and feelings about today:

Positive things that happened today:

How I felt today:

Happy	Inspired
Motivated	Optimistic
Creative	Excited
Focused	Hopeful
Reflective	

A goal for tomorrow:

"Make happiness a priority and be gentle with yourself in the process."

-Bronnie Ware

Morning Meditation

Date: /   /

todays focus:

_____

_____

_____

Affirmations for today:

_____

_____

_____

_____

Sleep I had last night:

Self-care to do today:

things I am grateful for today:

_____

_____

_____

_____

Evening Reflection

Date: / /

Positive thoughts and feelings about today:

Positive things that happened today:

How I felt today:

Happy	Inspired
Motivated	Optimistic
Creative	Excited
Focused	Hopeful
Reflective	

A goal for tomorrow:

Morning Meditation

todays focus:

_____

_____

_____

Affirmations for today:

_____

_____

_____

_____

Sleep I had last night:

Self-care to do today:

things I am grateful for today:

_____

_____

_____

_____

_____

Evening Reflection

Date: / /

Positive thoughts and feelings about today:

Positive things that happened today:

How I felt today:

Happy	Inspired
Motivated	Optimistic
Creative	Excited
Focused	Hopeful
Reflective	

A goal for tomorrow:

Morning Meditation

Date: / /

todays focus:

_____

_____

_____

Affirmations for today:

_____

_____

_____

_____

Sleep I had last night:

Self-care to do today:

things I am grateful for today:

_____

_____

_____

_____

_____

Evening Reflection

Date: / /

Positive thoughts and feelings about today:

Positive things that happened today:

How I felt today:

Happy	Inspired
Motivated	Optimistic
Creative	Excited
Focused	Hopeful
Reflective	

A goal for tomorrow:

Morning Meditation

Date: /   /

todays focus:

_____

_____

_____

Affirmations for today:

_____

_____

_____

_____

Sleep I had last night:

Self-care to do today:

things I am grateful for today:

_____

_____

_____

_____

_____

Evening Reflection

Date: / /

Positive thoughts and feelings about today:

Positive things that happened today:

How I felt today:

Happy	Inspired
Motivated	Optimistic
Creative	Excited
Focused	Hopeful
Reflective	

A goal for tomorrow:

Morning Meditation

Date: /   /

todays focus:

_____

_____

_____

Affirmations for today:

_____

_____

_____

_____

Sleep I had last night:

Self-care to do today:

things I am grateful for today:

_____

_____

_____

_____

Evening Reflection

Date: / /

Positive thoughts and feelings about today:

_____

_____

_____

_____

Positive things that happened today:

_____

_____

_____

_____

How I felt today:

Happy	Inspired
Motivated	Optimistic
Creative	Excited
Focused	Hopeful
Reflective	

A goal for tomorrow:

"You can't go back and change the beginning but you can start right now and change the ending."

-C. S. Lewis

Morning Meditation

Date: /   /

todays focus:

_____

_____

_____

Affirmations for today:

_____

_____

_____

_____

Sleep I had last night:

Self-care to do today:

things I am grateful for today:

_____

_____

_____

_____

_____

Evening Reflection

Date: / /

Positive thoughts and feelings about today:

_____

_____

_____

_____

Positive things that happened today:

_____

_____

_____

_____

How I felt today:

Happy	Inspired
Motivated	Optimistic
Creative	Excited
Focused	Hopeful
Reflective	

A goal for tomorrow:

Morning Meditation

Date: /   /

todays focus:

_____

_____

_____

Affirmations for today:

_____

_____

_____

_____

Sleep I had last night:

Self-care to do today:

things I am grateful for today:

_____

_____

_____

_____

_____

Evening Reflection

Date: / /

Positive thoughts and feelings about today:

_____

_____

_____

_____

Positive things that happened today:

_____

_____

_____

_____

How I felt today:

Happy	Inspired
Motivated	Optimistic
Creative	Excited
Focused	Hopeful
Reflective	

A goal for tomorrow:

Morning Meditation

Date: /   /

todays focus:

_____

_____

_____

Affirmations for today:

_____

_____

_____

_____

Sleep I had last night:

Self-care to do today:

things I am grateful for today:

_____

_____

_____

_____

_____

Evening Reflection

Date: / /

Positive thoughts and feelings about today:

Positive things that happened today:

How I felt today:

Happy	Inspired
Motivated	Optimistic
Creative	Excited
Focused	Hopeful
Reflective	

A goal for tomorrow:

Morning Meditation

Date: / /

todays focus:

_____
_____
_____

Affirmations for today:

_____
_____
_____
_____

Sleep I had last night:

Self-care to do today:

things I am grateful for today:

_____
_____
_____
_____
_____

Evening Reflection

Date: / /

Positive thoughts and feelings about today:

Positive things that happened today:

How I felt today:

Happy	Inspired
Motivated	Optimistic
Creative	Excited
Focused	Hopeful
Reflective	

A goal for tomorrow:

Morning Meditation

Date: / /

todays focus:

_____

_____

_____

Affirmations for today:

_____

_____

_____

_____

Sleep I had last night:

Self-care to do today:

things I am grateful for today:

_____

_____

_____

_____

Evening Reflection

Date: / /

Positive thoughts and feelings about today:

_____

_____

_____

_____

Positive things that happened today:

_____

_____

_____

_____

How I felt today:

Happy	Inspired
Motivated	Optimistic
Creative	Excited
Focused	Hopeful
Reflective	

A goal for tomorrow:

"Change your thoughts and you change your world."

-Norman Vincent Peale

Morning Meditation

Date: / /

todays focus:

_____
_____
_____

Affirmations for today:

_____
_____
_____
_____

Sleep I had last night:

Self-care to do today:

things I am grateful for today:

_____
_____
_____
_____

Evening Reflection

Date: / /

Positive thoughts and feelings about today:

_____

_____

_____

_____

Positive things that happened today:

_____

_____

_____

_____

How I felt today:

Happy	Inspired
Motivated	Optimistic
Creative	Excited
Focused	Hopeful
Reflective	

A goal for tomorrow:

Morning Meditation

Date: /   /

todays focus:

_____

_____

_____

Affirmations for today:

_____

_____

_____

_____

Sleep I had last night:

Self-care to do today:

things I am grateful for today:

_____

_____

_____

_____

Evening Reflection

Date: / /

Positive thoughts and feelings about today:

_____

_____

_____

_____

Positive things that happened today:

_____

_____

_____

_____

_____

How I felt today:

Happy	Inspired
Motivated	Optimistic
Creative	Excited
Focused	Hopeful
Reflective	

A goal for tomorrow:

Morning Meditation

Date: / /

todays focus:

_____

_____

_____

Affirmations for today:

_____

_____

_____

_____

Sleep I had last night:

Self-care to do today:

things I am grateful for today:

_____

_____

_____

_____

_____

Evening Reflection

Date: / /

Positive thoughts and feelings about today:

_____
_____
_____
_____

Positive things that happened today:

_____
_____
_____
_____
_____

How I felt today:

Happy	Inspired
Motivated	Optimistic
Creative	Excited
Focused	Hopeful
Reflective	

A goal for tomorrow:

Morning Meditation

Date: / /

todays focus:

_____

_____

_____

Affirmations for today:

_____

_____

_____

_____

Sleep I had last night:

Self-care to do today:

things I am grateful for today:

_____

_____

_____

_____

Evening Reflection

Date: / /

Positive thoughts and feelings about today:

Positive things that happened today:

How I felt today:

Happy	Inspired
Motivated	Optimistic
Creative	Excited
Focused	Hopeful
Reflective	

A goal for tomorrow:

Morning Meditation

Date: / /

todays focus:

_____

_____

_____

Affirmations for today:

_____

_____

_____

_____

Sleep I had last night:

Self-care to do today:

things I am grateful for today:

_____

_____

_____

_____

Evening Reflection

Date: / /

Positive thoughts and feelings about today:

Positive things that happened today:

How I felt today:

Happy	Inspired
Motivated	Optimistic
Creative	Excited
Focused	Hopeful
Reflective	

A goal for tomorrow:

"Gratitude is the single most important ingredient to living a successful and fulfilled life."

-Jack Cranfield

Morning Meditation

Date: / /

todays focus:

_____

_____

_____

Affirmations for today:

_____

_____

_____

_____

Sleep I had last night:

Self-care to do today:

things I am grateful for today:

_____

_____

_____

_____

_____

Evening Reflection

Date: / /

Positive thoughts and feelings about today:

_____

_____

_____

_____

Positive things that happened today:

_____

_____

_____

_____

How I felt today:

Happy	Inspired
Motivated	Optimistic
Creative	Excited
Focused	Hopeful
Reflective	

A goal for tomorrow:

Morning Meditation

Date: /   /

todays focus:

_____

_____

_____

Affirmations for today:

_____

_____

_____

_____

Sleep I had last night:

Self-care to do today:

things I am grateful for today:

_____

_____

_____

_____

Evening Reflection

Date: / /

Positive thoughts and feelings about today:

Positive things that happened today:

How I felt today:

Happy	Inspired
Motivated	Optimistic
Creative	Excited
Focused	Hopeful
Reflective	

A goal for tomorrow:

Morning Meditation

Date: / /

todays focus:

_____

_____

_____

Affirmations for today:

_____

_____

_____

_____

Sleep I had last night:

Self-care to do today:

things I am grateful for today:

_____

_____

_____

_____

_____

Evening Reflection

Date: / /

Positive thoughts and feelings about today:

_____

_____

_____

_____

Positive things that happened today:

_____

_____

_____

_____

_____

How I felt today:

Happy	Inspired
Motivated	Optimistic
Creative	Excited
Focused	Hopeful
Reflective	

A goal for tomorrow:

Morning Meditation

Date: / /

todays focus:

Affirmations for today:

Sleep I had last night:

Self-care to do today:

Things I am grateful for today:

Evening Reflection

Date: / /

Positive thoughts and feelings about today:

Positive things that happened today:

How I felt today:

Happy	Inspired
Motivated	Optimistic
Creative	Excited
Focused	Hopeful
Reflective	

A goal for tomorrow:

Morning Meditation

Date: / /

todays focus:

_____

_____

_____

Affirmations for today:

_____

_____

_____

_____

Sleep I had last night:

Self-care to do today:

things I am grateful for today:

_____

_____

_____

_____

Evening Reflection

Date: / /

Positive thoughts and feelings about today:

Positive things that happened today:

How I felt today:

Happy	Inspired
Motivated	Optimistic
Creative	Excited
Focused	Hopeful
Reflective	

A goal for tomorrow:

"Gratitude unlocks the fullness of life. It turns what we have into enough and more."

-Melody Beattie

Morning Meditation

Date: /   /

todays focus:

Affirmations for today:

Sleep I had last night:

Self-care to do today:

things I am grateful for today:

Evening Reflection

Date: / /

Positive thoughts and feelings about today:

_____

_____

_____

Positive things that happened today:

_____

_____

_____

_____

How I felt today:

Happy	Inspired
Motivated	Optimistic
Creative	Excited
Focused	Hopeful
Reflective	

A goal for tomorrow:

Morning Meditation

Date: / /

Todays focus:

_____

_____

_____

Affirmations for today:

_____

_____

_____

_____

Sleep I had last night:

Self-care to do today:

Things I am grateful for today:

_____

_____

_____

_____

Evening Reflection

Date: / /

Positive thoughts and feelings about today:

Positive things that happened today:

How I felt today:

Happy	Inspired
Motivated	Optimistic
Creative	Excited
Focused	Hopeful
Reflective	

A goal for tomorrow:

Morning Meditation

Date: / /

todays focus:

_____

_____

_____

Affirmations for today:

_____

_____

_____

_____

Sleep I had last night:

Self-care to do today:

Things I am grateful for today:

_____

_____

_____

_____

Evening Reflection

Date: / /

Positive thoughts and feelings about today:

_____

_____

_____

_____

Positive things that happened today:

_____

_____

_____

_____

_____

How I felt today:

Happy	Inspired
Motivated	Optimistic
Creative	Excited
Focused	Hopeful
Reflective	

A goal for tomorrow:

Morning Meditation

Date: / /

Todays focus:

_____

_____

_____

Affirmations for today:

_____

_____

_____

_____

Sleep I had last night:

Self-care to do today:

Things I am grateful for today:

_____

_____

_____

_____

_____

Evening Reflection

Date: / /

Positive thoughts and feelings about today:

_____

_____

_____

_____

Positive things that happened today:

_____

_____

_____

_____

How I felt today:

Happy	Inspired
Motivated	Optimistic
Creative	Excited
Focused	Hopeful
Reflective	

A goal for tomorrow:

Morning Meditation

Date: /   /

todays focus:

_____
_____
_____

Affirmations for today:

_____
_____
_____

Sleep I had last night:

Self-care to do today:

Things I am grateful for today:

_____
_____
_____
_____
_____

Evening Reflection

Date: /   /

Positive thoughts and feelings about today:

_____

_____

_____

_____

Positive things that happened today:

_____

_____

_____

_____

_____

How I felt today:

Happy	Inspired
Motivated	Optimistic
Creative	Excited
Focused	Hopeful
Reflective	

A goal for tomorrow:

"Just as the sun encourages a tulip to open, we too can be opened by the act of gratitude."

-Sye Artus

Morning Meditation

Date: / /

todays focus:

_____

_____

_____

Affirmations for today:

_____

_____

_____

_____

Sleep I had last night:

Self-care to do today:

things I am grateful for today:

_____

_____

_____

_____

_____

Evening Reflection

Date: / /

Positive thoughts and feelings about today:

_____
_____
_____
_____

Positive things that happened today:

_____
_____
_____
_____

How I felt today:

Happy	Inspired
Motivated	Optimistic
Creative	Excited
Focused	Hopeful
Reflective	

A goal for tomorrow:

Morning Meditation

Date: /   /

todays focus:

_____

_____

_____

Affirmations for today:

_____

_____

_____

_____

Sleep I had last night:

Self-care to do today:

things I am grateful for today:

_____

_____

_____

_____

Evening Reflection

Date: / /

Positive thoughts and feelings about today:

Positive things that happened today:

How I felt today:

Happy	Inspired
Motivated	Optimistic
Creative	Excited
Focused	Hopeful
Reflective	

A goal for tomorrow:

Morning Meditation

Date: /   /

todays focus:

_____

_____

_____

Affirmations for today:

_____

_____

_____

_____

Sleep I had last night:

Self-care to do today:

things I am grateful for today:

_____

_____

_____

_____

_____

Evening Reflection

Date: / /

Positive thoughts and feelings about today:

Positive things that happened today:

How I felt today:

Happy	Inspired
Motivated	Optimistic
Creative	Excited
Focused	Hopeful
Reflective	

A goal for tomorrow:

Morning Meditation

Date: / /

todays focus:

_____
_____
_____

Affirmations for today:

_____
_____
_____
_____

Sleep I had last night:

Self-care to do today:

things I am grateful for today:

_____
_____
_____
_____
_____

Evening Reflection

Date: / /

Positive thoughts and feelings about today:

_____

_____

_____

_____

Positive things that happened today:

_____

_____

_____

_____

_____

How I felt today:

Happy	Inspired
Motivated	Optimistic
Creative	Excited
Focused	Hopeful
Reflective	

A goal for tomorrow:

Morning Meditation

Date: / /

todays focus:

_____

_____

_____

Affirmations for today:

_____

_____

_____

_____

Sleep I had last night:

Self-care to do today:

Things I am grateful for today:

_____

_____

_____

_____

_____

Evening Reflection

Date: / /

Positive thoughts and feelings about today:

_____

_____

_____

_____

Positive things that happened today:

_____

_____

_____

_____

How I felt today:

Happy	Inspired
Motivated	Optimistic
Creative	Excited
Focused	Hopeful
Reflective	

A goal for tomorrow:

"You become what you believe."

-Oprah Winfrey

Morning Meditation

Date: /   /

todays focus:

_____

_____

_____

Affirmations for today:

_____

_____

_____

_____

Sleep I had last night:

Self-care to do today:

things I am grateful for today:

_____

_____

_____

_____

_____

Evening Reflection

Date: / /

Positive thoughts and feelings about today:

_____

_____

_____

_____

Positive things that happened today:

_____

_____

_____

_____

How I felt today:

Happy	Inspired
Motivated	Optimistic
Creative	Excited
Focused	Hopeful
Reflective	

A goal for tomorrow:

Morning Meditation

Date: /   /

todays focus:

_____

_____

_____

Affirmations for today:

_____

_____

_____

_____

Sleep I had last night:

Self-care to do today:

things I am grateful for today:

_____

_____

_____

_____

Evening Reflection

Date: / /

Positive thoughts and feelings about today:

_____

_____

_____

_____

Positive things that happened today:

_____

_____

_____

_____

How I felt today:

Happy	Inspired
Motivated	Optimistic
Creative	Excited
Focused	Hopeful
Reflective	

A goal for tomorrow:

Morning Meditation

Date: / /

todays focus:

_____
_____
_____

Affirmations for today:

_____
_____
_____
_____

Sleep I had last night:

Self-care to do today:

things I am grateful for today:

_____
_____
_____
_____
_____

Evening Reflection

Date: / /

Positive thoughts and feelings about today:

_____

_____

_____

_____

Positive things that happened today:

_____

_____

_____

_____

_____

How I felt today:

Happy	Inspired
Motivated	Optimistic
Creative	Excited
Focused	Hopeful
Reflective	

A goal for tomorrow:

Morning Meditation

Date: / /

todays focus:

_____

_____

_____

Affirmations for today:

_____

_____

_____

_____

Sleep I had last night:

Self-care to do today:

things I am grateful for today:

_____

_____

_____

_____

_____

Evening Reflection

Date: / /

Positive thoughts and feelings about today:

_____

_____

_____

_____

Positive things that happened today:

_____

_____

_____

_____

How I felt today:

Happy	Inspired
Motivated	Optimistic
Creative	Excited
Focused	Hopeful
Reflective	

A goal for tomorrow:

Morning Meditation

Date: / /

todays focus:

_____

_____

_____

Affirmations for today:

_____

_____

_____

_____

Sleep I had last night:

Self-care to do today:

things I am grateful for today:

_____

_____

_____

_____

_____

Evening Reflection

Date: / /

Positive thoughts and feelings about today:

Positive things that happened today:

How I felt today:

Happy	Inspired
Motivated	Optimistic
Creative	Excited
Focused	Hopeful
Reflective	

A goal for tomorrow:

"The best way to pursue happiness is to help other people. Nothing else will make you happier."

-George Lucas

Morning Meditation

Date: / /

todays focus:

_____

_____

_____

Affirmations for today:

_____

_____

_____

_____

Sleep I had last night:

Self-care to do today:

things I am grateful for today:

_____

_____

_____

_____

_____

Evening Reflection

Date: / /

Positive thoughts and feelings about today:

_____

_____

_____

_____

Positive things that happened today:

_____

_____

_____

_____

_____

How I felt today:

Happy	Inspired
Motivated	Optimistic
Creative	Excited
Focused	Hopeful
Reflective	

A goal for tomorrow:

Morning Meditation

Date: /   /

todays focus:

_____

_____

_____

Affirmations for today:

_____

_____

_____

_____

Sleep I had last night:

Self-care to do today:

things I am grateful for today:

_____

_____

_____

_____

_____

Evening Reflection

Date: / /

Positive thoughts and feelings about today:

Positive things that happened today:

How I felt today:

Happy	Inspired
Motivated	Optimistic
Creative	Excited
Focused	Hopeful
Reflective	

A goal for tomorrow:

Morning Meditation

Date: / /

todays focus:

_____

_____

_____

Affirmations for today:

_____

_____

_____

_____

Sleep I had last night:

Self-care to do today:

things I am grateful for today:

_____

_____

_____

_____

_____

Evening Reflection

Date: / /

Positive thoughts and feelings about today:

_____

_____

_____

_____

Positive things that happened today:

_____

_____

_____

_____

_____

How I felt today:

Happy	Inspired
Motivated	Optimistic
Creative	Excited
Focused	Hopeful
Reflective	

A goal for tomorrow:

Morning Meditation

Date: / /

todays focus:

_____

_____

_____

Affirmations for today:

_____

_____

_____

_____

Sleep I had last night:

Self-care to do today:

things I am grateful for today:

_____

_____

_____

_____

Evening Reflection

Date: / /

Positive thoughts and feelings about today:

Positive things that happened today:

How I felt today:

Happy	Inspired
Motivated	Optimistic
Creative	Excited
Focused	Hopeful
Reflective	

A goal for tomorrow:

Morning Meditation

Date: /   /

todays focus:

_____

_____

_____

Affirmations for today:

_____

_____

_____

_____

Sleep I had last night:

Self-care to do today:

things I am grateful for today:

_____

_____

_____

_____

_____

Evening Reflection

Date: / /

Positive thoughts and feelings about today:

_____

_____

_____

Positive things that happened today:

_____

_____

_____

_____

How I felt today:

Happy	Inspired
Motivated	Optimistic
Creative	Excited
Focused	Hopeful
Reflective	

A goal for tomorrow:

"You can have, do or be anything you want."

-Dr Joe Vitale

Morning Meditation

Date: / /

todays focus:

_____
_____
_____

Affirmations for today:

_____
_____
_____
_____

Sleep I had last night:

Self-care to do today:

things I am grateful for today:

_____
_____
_____
_____
_____

Evening Reflection

Date: / /

Positive thoughts and feelings about today:

_____

_____

_____

_____

Positive things that happened today:

_____

_____

_____

_____

How I felt today:

Happy	Inspired
Motivated	Optimistic
Creative	Excited
Focused	Hopeful
Reflective	

A goal for tomorrow:

Morning Meditation

Date: / /

todays focus:

_____

_____

_____

Affirmations for today:

_____

_____

_____

_____

Sleep I had last night:

Self-care to do today:

things I am grateful for today:

_____

_____

_____

_____

_____

Evening Reflection

Date: / /

Positive thoughts and feelings about today:

_____

_____

_____

_____

Positive things that happened today:

_____

_____

_____

_____

_____

How I felt today:

Happy	Inspired
Motivated	Optimistic
Creative	Excited
Focused	Hopeful
Reflective	

A goal for tomorrow:

Morning Meditation

Date: / /

todays focus:

_____

_____

_____

Affirmations for today:

_____

_____

_____

_____

Sleep I had last night:

Self-care to do today:

things I am grateful for today:

_____

_____

_____

_____

_____

Evening Reflection

Date: / /

Positive thoughts and feelings about today:

Positive things that happened today:

How I felt today:

Happy	Inspired
Motivated	Optimistic
Creative	Excited
Focused	Hopeful
Reflective	

A goal for tomorrow:

Morning Meditation

Date: / /

todays focus:

_____

_____

_____

Affirmations for today:

_____

_____

_____

_____

Sleep I had last night:

Self-care to do today:

things I am grateful for today:

_____

_____

_____

_____

_____

Evening Reflection

Date: / /

Positive thoughts and feelings about today:

Positive things that happened today:

How I felt today:

Happy	Inspired
Motivated	Optimistic
Creative	Excited
Focused	Hopeful
Reflective	

A goal for tomorrow:

Morning Meditation

Date: / /

todays focus:

_____

_____

_____

Affirmations for today:

_____

_____

_____

_____

Sleep I had last night:

Self-care to do today:

things I am grateful for today:

_____

_____

_____

_____

_____

Evening Reflection

Date: / /

Positive thoughts and feelings about today:

_____

_____

_____

Positive things that happened today:

_____

_____

_____

_____

How I felt today:

Happy	Inspired
Motivated	Optimistic
Creative	Excited
Focused	Hopeful
Reflective	

A goal for tomorrow:

"Imagination is everything. It is the preview of life's coming attractions."

-Albert Einstein

Morning Meditation

Date: /   /

todays focus:

_____

_____

_____

Affirmations for today:

_____

_____

_____

_____

Sleep I had last night:

Self-care to do today:

things I am grateful for today:

_____

_____

_____

_____

Evening Reflection

Date: / /

Positive thoughts and feelings about today:

_____
_____
_____

Positive things that happened today:

_____
_____
_____
_____

How I felt today:

Happy	Inspired
Motivated	Optimistic
Creative	Excited
Focused	Hopeful
Reflective	

A goal for tomorrow:

Morning Meditation

Date: / /

todays focus:

_____

_____

_____

Affirmations for today:

_____

_____

_____

_____

Sleep I had last night:

Self-care to do today:

Things I am grateful for today:

_____

_____

_____

_____

_____

Evening Reflection

Date: / /

Positive thoughts and feelings about today:

_____

_____

_____

_____

Positive things that happened today:

_____

_____

_____

_____

_____

How I felt today:

Happy	Inspired
Motivated	Optimistic
Creative	Excited
Focused	Hopeful
Reflective	

A goal for tomorrow:

Morning Meditation

Date: / /

Todays focus:

_____

_____

_____

Affirmations for today:

_____

_____

_____

_____

Sleep I had last night:

Self-care to do today:

Things I am grateful for today:

_____

_____

_____

_____

_____

Evening Reflection

Date: / /

Positive thoughts and feelings about today:

Positive things that happened today:

How I felt today:

Happy	Inspired
Motivated	Optimistic
Creative	Excited
Focused	Hopeful
Reflective	

A goal for tomorrow:

Morning Meditation

Date: /   /

todays focus:

_____

_____

_____

Affirmations for today:

_____

_____

_____

_____

Sleep I had last night:

Self-care to do today:

things I am grateful for today:

_____

_____

_____

_____

_____

Evening Reflection

Date: / /

Positive thoughts and feelings about today:

_____

_____

_____

_____

Positive things that happened today:

_____

_____

_____

_____

_____

How I felt today:

Happy	Inspired
Motivated	Optimistic
Creative	Excited
Focused	Hopeful
Reflective	

A goal for tomorrow:

Morning Meditation

Date: / /

todays focus:

_____

_____

_____

Affirmations for today:

_____

_____

_____

_____

Sleep I had last night:

Self-care to do today:

things I am grateful for today:

_____

_____

_____

_____

Evening Reflection

Date: / /

Positive thoughts and feelings about today:

_____

_____

_____

_____

Positive things that happened today:

_____

_____

_____

_____

_____

How I felt today:

Happy	Inspired
Motivated	Optimistic
Creative	Excited
Focused	Hopeful
Reflective	

A goal for tomorrow:

"Keep your mind fixed on what you want in life: not on what you don't want."

-Napoleon Hill

Morning Meditation

Date: /   /

Todays focus:

_____

_____

_____

Affirmations for today:

_____

_____

_____

_____

Sleep I had last night:

Self-care to do today:

Things I am grateful for today:

_____

_____

_____

_____

Evening Reflection

Date: / /

Positive thoughts and feelings about today:

_____

_____

_____

_____

Positive things that happened today:

_____

_____

_____

_____

How I felt today:

Happy	Inspired
Motivated	Optimistic
Creative	Excited
Focused	Hopeful
Reflective	

A goal for tomorrow:

Morning Meditation

Date: /   /

Todays focus:

_____

_____

_____

Affirmations for today:

_____

_____

_____

_____

Sleep I had last night:

Self-care to do today:

things I am grateful for today:

_____

_____

_____

_____

_____

Evening Reflection

Date: / /

Positive thoughts and feelings about today:

_____

_____

_____

_____

Positive things that happened today:

_____

_____

_____

_____

How I felt today:

Happy	Inspired
Motivated	Optimistic
Creative	Excited
Focused	Hopeful
Reflective	

A goal for tomorrow:

Morning Meditation

Date: / /

todays focus:

_____

_____

_____

Affirmations for today:

_____

_____

_____

_____

Sleep I had last night:

Self-care to do today:

things I am grateful for today:

_____

_____

_____

_____

Evening Reflection

Date: / /

Positive thoughts and feelings about today:

Positive things that happened today:

How I felt today:

Happy	Inspired
Motivated	Optimistic
Creative	Excited
Focused	Hopeful
Reflective	

A goal for tomorrow:

Morning Meditation

Date: / /

todays focus:

_____

_____

_____

Affirmations for today:

_____

_____

_____

_____

Sleep I had last night:

Self-care to do today:

things I am grateful for today:

_____

_____

_____

_____

_____

Evening Reflection

Date: / /

Positive thoughts and feelings about today:

Positive things that happened today:

How I felt today:

Happy	Inspired
Motivated	Optimistic
Creative	Excited
Focused	Hopeful
Reflective	

A goal for tomorrow:

Morning Meditation

Date: / /

todays focus:

_____

_____

_____

Affirmations for today:

_____

_____

_____

_____

Sleep I had last night:

Self-care to do today:

things I am grateful for today:

_____

_____

_____

_____

_____

Evening Reflection

Date: / /

Positive thoughts and feelings about today:

Positive things that happened today:

How I felt today:

Happy	Inspired
Motivated	Optimistic
Creative	Excited
Focused	Hopeful
Reflective	

A goal for tomorrow:

"We do not need magic to transform our world. We carry all the power we need inside ourselves already."

-J. K. Rowling

Morning Meditation

Date: / /

todays focus:

_____
_____
_____

Affirmations for today:

_____
_____
_____
_____

Sleep I had last night:

Self-care to do today:

things I am grateful for today:

_____
_____
_____
_____

Evening Reflection

Date: / /

Positive thoughts and feelings about today:

_____

_____

_____

_____

Positive things that happened today:

_____

_____

_____

_____

_____

How I felt today:

Happy	Inspired
Motivated	Optimistic
Creative	Excited
Focused	Hopeful
Reflective	

A goal for tomorrow:

Morning Meditation

Date: /   /

todays focus:

_____
_____

_____

Affirmations for today:

_____

_____

_____

_____

Sleep I had last night:

Self-care to do today:

Things I am grateful for today:

_____

_____

_____

_____

_____

Evening Reflection

Date: / /

Positive thoughts and feelings about today:

_____

_____

_____

_____

Positive things that happened today:

_____

_____

_____

_____

How I felt today:

Happy	Inspired
Motivated	Optimistic
Creative	Excited
Focused	Hopeful
Reflective	

A goal for tomorrow:

Morning Meditation

Date: / /

todays focus:

_____

_____

_____

Affirmations for today:

_____

_____

_____

_____

Sleep I had last night:

Self-care to do today:

things I am grateful for today:

_____

_____

_____

_____

_____

Evening Reflection

Date: / /

Positive thoughts and feelings about today:

_____

_____

_____

_____

Positive things that happened today:

_____

_____

_____

_____

How I felt today:

Happy	Inspired
Motivated	Optimistic
Creative	Excited
Focused	Hopeful
Reflective	

A goal for tomorrow:

Morning Meditation

Date: / /

Todays focus:

_____

_____

_____

Affirmations for today:

_____

_____

_____

_____

Sleep I had last night:

Self-care to do today:

Things I am grateful for today:

_____

_____

_____

_____

Evening Reflection

Date: / /

Positive thoughts and feelings about today:

_____

_____

_____

_____

Positive things that happened today:

_____

_____

_____

_____

_____

How I felt today:

Happy	Inspired
Motivated	Optimistic
Creative	Excited
Focused	Hopeful
Reflective	

A goal for tomorrow:

Morning Meditation

Date: / /

todays focus:

_____

_____

_____

Affirmations for today:

_____

_____

_____

_____

Sleep I had last night:

Self-care to do today:

things I am grateful for today:

_____

_____

_____

_____

Evening Reflection

Date: / /

Positive thoughts and feelings about today:

_____

_____

_____

_____

Positive things that happened today:

_____

_____

_____

_____

_____

How I felt today:

Happy	Inspired
Motivated	Optimistic
Creative	Excited
Focused	Hopeful
Reflective	

A goal for tomorrow:

"Once you replace negative thoughts with positive ones you'll start having positive results."

-Willie Nelson

Morning Meditation

Date: / /

todays focus:

_____

_____

_____

Affirmations for today:

_____

_____

_____

_____

Sleep I had last night:

Self-care to do today:

things I am grateful for today:

_____

_____

_____

_____

Evening Reflection

Date: / /

Positive thoughts and feelings about today:

Positive things that happened today:

How I felt today:

Happy	Inspired
Motivated	Optimistic
Creative	Excited
Focused	Hopeful
Reflective	

A goal for tomorrow:

Morning Meditation

Date: / /

todays focus:

_____

_____

_____

Affirmations for today:

_____

_____

_____

_____

Sleep I had last night:

Self-care to do today:

things I am grateful for today:

_____

_____

_____

_____

_____

Evening Reflection

Date: / /

Positive thoughts and feelings about today:

_____

_____

_____

_____

Positive things that happened today:

_____

_____

_____

_____

How I felt today:

Happy	Inspired
Motivated	Optimistic
Creative	Excited
Focused	Hopeful
Reflective	

A goal for tomorrow:

Morning Meditation

Date: / /

todays focus:

_____

_____

_____

Affirmations for today:

_____

_____

_____

_____

Sleep I had last night:

Self-care to do today:

things I am grateful for today:

_____

_____

_____

_____

Evening Reflection

Date: / /

Positive thoughts and feelings about today:

_____
_____
_____
_____

Positive things that happened today:

_____
_____
_____
_____

How I felt today:

Happy	Inspired
Motivated	Optimistic
Creative	Excited
Focused	Hopeful
Reflective	

A goal for tomorrow:

Morning Meditation

Date: / /

todays focus:

_____
_____
_____

Affirmations for today:

_____
_____
_____
_____

Sleep I had last night:

Self-care to do today:

things I am grateful for today:

_____
_____
_____
_____

Evening Reflection

Date: / /

Positive thoughts and feelings about today:

Positive things that happened today:

How I felt today:

Happy	Inspired
Motivated	Optimistic
Creative	Excited
Focused	Hopeful
Reflective	

A goal for tomorrow:

Morning Meditation

Date: / /

todays focus:

_____

_____

_____

Affirmations for today:

_____

_____

_____

_____

Sleep I had last night:

Self-care to do today:

things I am grateful for today:

_____

_____

_____

_____

_____

Evening Reflection

Date: / /

Positive thoughts and feelings about today:

_____

_____

_____

_____

Positive things that happened today:

_____

_____

_____

_____

How I felt today:

Happy	Inspired
Motivated	Optimistic
Creative	Excited
Focused	Hopeful
Reflective	

A goal for tomorrow:

"Every thought we think is creating our future."

-Louise L. Hay

Morning Meditation

Date: / /

todays focus:

_____

_____

_____

Affirmations for today:

_____

_____

_____

_____

Sleep I had last night:

Self-care to do today:

things I am grateful for today:

_____

_____

_____

_____

_____

Evening Reflection

Date: /   /

Positive thoughts and feelings about today:

Positive things that happened today:

How I felt today:

Happy	Inspired
Motivated	Optimistic
Creative	Excited
Focused	Hopeful
Reflective	

A goal for tomorrow:

Morning Meditation

Date: / /

todays focus:

_____
_____
_____

Affirmations for today:

_____
_____
_____
_____

Sleep I had last night:

Self-care to do today:

things I am grateful for today:

_____
_____
_____
_____
_____

Evening Reflection

Date: / /

Positive thoughts and feelings about today:

_____

_____

_____

_____

Positive things that happened today:

_____

_____

_____

_____

How I felt today:

Happy	Inspired
Motivated	Optimistic
Creative	Excited
Focused	Hopeful
Reflective	

A goal for tomorrow:

Morning Meditation

Date: /   /

todays focus:

_____

_____

_____

Affirmations for today:

_____

_____

_____

_____

Sleep I had last night:

Self-care to do today:

things I am grateful for today:

_____

_____

_____

_____

_____

Evening Reflection

Date: /   /

Positive thoughts and feelings about today:

_____

_____

_____

_____

Positive things that happened today:

_____

_____

_____

_____

How I felt today:

Happy	Inspired
Motivated	Optimistic
Creative	Excited
Focused	Hopeful
Reflective	

A goal for tomorrow:

Morning Meditation

Date: / /

todays focus:

_____

_____

_____

Affirmations for today:

_____

_____

_____

_____

Sleep I had last night:

Self-care to do today:

things I am grateful for today:

_____

_____

_____

_____

_____

Evening Reflection

Date: / /

Positive thoughts and feelings about today:

_____

_____

_____

_____

Positive things that happened today:

_____

_____

_____

_____

_____

How I felt today:

Happy	Inspired
Motivated	Optimistic
Creative	Excited
Focused	Hopeful
Reflective	

A goal for tomorrow:

Morning Meditation

Date: /   /

todays focus:

_____

_____

_____

Affirmations for today:

_____

_____

_____

_____

Sleep I had last night:

Self-care to do today:

things I am grateful for today:

_____

_____

_____

_____

_____

Evening Reflection

Date: / /

Positive thoughts and feelings about today:

_____

_____

_____

_____

Positive things that happened today:

_____

_____

_____

_____

How I felt today:

Happy	Inspired
Motivated	Optimistic
Creative	Excited
Focused	Hopeful
Reflective	

A goal for tomorrow:

"Follow your bliss and the Universe will open doors for you where there were only walls."

-Joseph Campbell

Morning Meditation

Date: / /

todays focus:

_____

_____

_____

Affirmations for today:

_____

_____

_____

_____

Sleep I had last night:

Self-care to do today:

things I am grateful for today:

_____

_____

_____

_____

_____

Evening Reflection

Date: / /

Positive thoughts and feelings about today:

Positive things that happened today:

How I felt today:

Happy	Inspired
Motivated	Optimistic
Creative	Excited
Focused	Hopeful
Reflective	

A goal for tomorrow:

Morning Meditation

Date: / /

todays focus:

_____
_____
_____

Affirmations for today:

_____
_____
_____
_____

Sleep I had last night:

Self-care to do today:

things I am grateful for today:

_____
_____
_____
_____

Evening Reflection

Date: / /

Positive thoughts and feelings about today:

_____

_____

_____

_____

Positive things that happened today:

_____

_____

_____

_____

_____

How I felt today:

Happy	Inspired
Motivated	Optimistic
Creative	Excited
Focused	Hopeful
Reflective	

A goal for tomorrow:

Morning Meditation

Date: / /

todays focus:

_____

_____

_____

Affirmations for today:

_____

_____

_____

_____

Sleep I had last night:

Self-care to do today:

things I am grateful for today:

_____

_____

_____

_____

Evening Reflection

Date: / /

Positive thoughts and feelings about today:

_____

_____

_____

_____

Positive things that happened today:

_____

_____

_____

_____

_____

How I felt today:

Happy	Inspired
Motivated	Optimistic
Creative	Excited
Focused	Hopeful
Reflective	

A goal for tomorrow:

Morning Meditation

Date: / /

todays focus:

_____

_____

_____

Affirmations for today:

_____

_____

_____

_____

Sleep I had last night:

Self-care to do today:

Things I am grateful for today:

_____

_____

_____

_____

Evening Reflection

Date: / /

Positive thoughts and feelings about today:

_____

_____

_____

_____

Positive things that happened today:

_____

_____

_____

_____

_____

How I felt today:

Happy	Inspired
Motivated	Optimistic
Creative	Excited
Focused	Hopeful
Reflective	

A goal for tomorrow:

Morning Meditation

Date: /   /

todays focus:

_____

_____

_____

Affirmations for today:

_____

_____

_____

_____

Sleep I had last night:

Self-care to do today:

things I am grateful for today:

_____

_____

_____

_____

Evening Reflection

Date: / /

Positive thoughts and feelings about today:

_____

_____

_____

_____

Positive things that happened today:

_____

_____

_____

_____

_____

How I felt today:

Happy	Inspired
Motivated	Optimistic
Creative	Excited
Focused	Hopeful
Reflective	

A goal for tomorrow:

"Your whole life is a manifestation of the thoughts that go on in your head."

-Lisa Nichols

Morning Meditation

Date: / /

todays focus:

_____

_____

_____

Affirmations for today:

_____

_____

_____

_____

Sleep I had last night:

Self-care to do today:

things I am grateful for today:

_____

_____

_____

_____

Evening Reflection

Date: / /

Positive thoughts and feelings about today:

_____

_____

_____

_____

Positive things that happened today:

_____

_____

_____

_____

How I felt today:

Happy	Inspired
Motivated	Optimistic
Creative	Excited
Focused	Hopeful
Reflective	

A goal for tomorrow:

Morning Meditation

Date: / /

todays focus:

_____

_____

_____

Affirmations for today:

_____

_____

_____

_____

Sleep I had last night:

Self-care to do today:

things I am grateful for today:

_____

_____

_____

_____

_____

Evening Reflection

Date: / /

Positive thoughts and feelings about today:

_____

_____

_____

_____

Positive things that happened today:

_____

_____

_____

_____

_____

How I felt today:

Happy	Inspired
Motivated	Optimistic
Creative	Excited
Focused	Hopeful
Reflective	

A goal for tomorrow:

Morning Meditation

Date: / /

todays focus:

_____

_____

_____

Affirmations for today:

_____

_____

_____

_____

Sleep I had last night:

Self-care to do today:

things I am grateful for today:

_____

_____

_____

_____

_____

Evening Reflection

Date: / /

Positive thoughts and feelings about today:

Positive things that happened today:

How I felt today:

Happy	Inspired
Motivated	Optimistic
Creative	Excited
Focused	Hopeful
Reflective	

A goal for tomorrow:

Morning Meditation

Date: / /

todays focus:

_____

_____

_____

Affirmations for today:

_____

_____

_____

_____

Sleep I had last night:

Self-care to do today:

things I am grateful for today:

_____

_____

_____

_____

_____

Evening Reflection

Date: / /

Positive thoughts and feelings about today:

_____

_____

_____

_____

Positive things that happened today:

_____

_____

_____

_____

_____

How I felt today:

Happy	Inspired
Motivated	Optimistic
Creative	Excited
Focused	Hopeful
Reflective	

A goal for tomorrow:

Morning Meditation

Date: / /

todays focus:

_____

_____

_____

Affirmations for today:

_____

_____

_____

_____

Sleep I had last night:

Self-care to do today:

things I am grateful for today:

_____

_____

_____

_____

Evening Reflection

Date: / /

Positive thoughts and feelings about today:

Positive things that happened today:

How I felt today:

Happy	Inspired
Motivated	Optimistic
Creative	Excited
Focused	Hopeful
Reflective	

A goal for tomorrow:

"Very little is needed to make a happy life, it is all within yourself, in your way of thinking."

-Marcus Aurelius

Morning Meditation

Date: / /

todays focus:

_____

_____

_____

Affirmations for today:

_____

_____

_____

_____

Sleep I had last night:

Self-care to do today:

things I am grateful for today:

_____

_____

_____

_____

Evening Reflection

Date: / /

Positive thoughts and feelings about today:

_____

_____

_____

_____

Positive things that happened today:

_____

_____

_____

_____

_____

How I felt today:

Happy	Inspired
Motivated	Optimistic
Creative	Excited
Focused	Hopeful
Reflective	

A goal for tomorrow:

Morning Meditation

Date: / /

Todays focus:

Affirmations for today:

Sleep I had last night:

Self-care to do today:

Things I am grateful for today:

Evening Reflection

Date: / /

Positive thoughts and feelings about today:

Positive things that happened today:

How I felt today:

Happy	Inspired
Motivated	Optimistic
Creative	Excited
Focused	Hopeful
Reflective	

A goal for tomorrow:

Morning Meditation

Date: / /

todays focus:

_____

_____

_____

Affirmations for today:

_____

_____

_____

_____

Sleep I had last night:

Self-care to do today:

things I am grateful for today:

_____

_____

_____

_____

_____

Evening Reflection

Date: / /

Positive thoughts and feelings about today:

_____

_____

_____

_____

Positive things that happened today:

_____

_____

_____

_____

How I felt today:

Happy	Inspired
Motivated	Optimistic
Creative	Excited
Focused	Hopeful
Reflective	

A goal for tomorrow:

Morning Meditation

Date: /   /

todays focus:

_____

_____

_____

Affirmations for today:

_____

_____

_____

_____

Sleep I had last night:

Self-care to do today:

things I am grateful for today:

_____

_____

_____

_____

_____

Evening Reflection

Date: / /

Positive thoughts and feelings about today:

_____

_____

_____

_____

Positive things that happened today:

_____

_____

_____

_____

_____

How I felt today:

Happy	Inspired
Motivated	Optimistic
Creative	Excited
Focused	Hopeful
Reflective	

A goal for tomorrow:

Morning Meditation

Date: / /

todays focus:

_____

_____

_____

Affirmations for today:

_____

_____

_____

_____

Sleep I had last night:

Self-care to do today:

things I am grateful for today:

_____

_____

_____

_____

Evening Reflection

Date: / /

Positive thoughts and feelings about today:

_____

_____

_____

_____

Positive things that happened today:

_____

_____

_____

_____

_____

How I felt today:

Happy	Inspired
Motivated	Optimistic
Creative	Excited
Focused	Hopeful
Reflective	

A goal for tomorrow:

"The idea is the first currency of the Universe, so pay attention to the ideas that are in harmony with your vision."

-Mary Morrissey

Morning Meditation

Date: / /

todays focus:

_____

_____

_____

Affirmations for today:

_____

_____

_____

_____

Sleep I had last night:

Self-care to do today:

things I am grateful for today:

_____

_____

_____

_____

Evening Reflection

Date: / /

Positive thoughts and feelings about today:

_____
_____
_____
_____

Positive things that happened today:

_____
_____
_____
_____
_____

How I felt today:

Happy	Inspired
Motivated	Optimistic
Creative	Excited
Focused	Hopeful
Reflective	

A goal for tomorrow:

Morning Meditation

Date: / /

todays focus:

_____
_____
_____

Affirmations for today:

_____
_____
_____
_____

Sleep I had last night:

Self-care to do today:

things I am grateful for today:

_____
_____
_____
_____
_____

Evening Reflection

Date: / /

Positive thoughts and feelings about today:

_____
_____
_____
_____

Positive things that happened today:

_____
_____
_____
_____
_____

How I felt today:

Happy	Inspired
Motivated	Optimistic
Creative	Excited
Focused	Hopeful
Reflective	

A goal for tomorrow:

Morning Meditation

Date: / /

todays focus:

_____

_____

_____

Affirmations for today:

_____

_____

_____

_____

Sleep I had last night:

Self-care to do today:

Things I am grateful for today:

_____

_____

_____

_____

_____

Evening Reflection

Date: / /

Positive thoughts and feelings about today:

_____

_____

_____

_____

Positive things that happened today:

_____

_____

_____

_____

How I felt today:

Happy	Inspired
Motivated	Optimistic
Creative	Excited
Focused	Hopeful
Reflective	

A goal for tomorrow:

Morning Meditation

Date: / /

todays focus:

_____

_____

_____

Affirmations for today:

_____

_____

_____

_____

Sleep I had last night:

Self-care to do today:

things I am grateful for today:

_____

_____

_____

_____

_____

Evening Reflection

Date: / /

Positive thoughts and feelings about today:

_____

_____

_____

_____

Positive things that happened today:

_____

_____

_____

_____

How I felt today:

Happy	Inspired
Motivated	Optimistic
Creative	Excited
Focused	Hopeful
Reflective	

A goal for tomorrow:

Morning Meditation

Date: / /

todays focus:

_____
_____
_____

Affirmations for today:

_____
_____
_____
_____

Sleep I had last night:

Self-care to do today:

things I am grateful for today:

_____
_____
_____
_____
_____

Evening Reflection

Date: / /

Positive thoughts and feelings about today:

_____

_____

_____

_____

Positive things that happened today:

_____

_____

_____

_____

How I felt today:

Happy	Inspired
Motivated	Optimistic
Creative	Excited
Focused	Hopeful
Reflective	

A goal for tomorrow:

"With every new day comes new strength and new thoughts."

-Eleanor Roosevelt

Morning Meditation

Date: /   /

todays focus:

_____

_____

_____

Affirmations for today:

_____

_____

_____

_____

Sleep I had last night:

Self-care to do today:

things I am grateful for today:

_____

_____

_____

_____

_____

Evening Reflection

Date: / /

Positive thoughts and feelings about today:

_____
_____
_____
_____

Positive things that happened today:

_____
_____
_____
_____
_____

How I felt today:

Happy	Inspired
Motivated	Optimistic
Creative	Excited
Focused	Hopeful
Reflective	

A goal for tomorrow:

Morning Meditation

todays focus:

_____
_____
_____

Affirmations for today:

_____
_____
_____
_____

Sleep I had last night:

Self-care to do today:

things I am grateful for today:

_____
_____
_____
_____
_____

Evening Reflection

Date: /   /

Positive thoughts and feelings about today:

_____

_____

_____

_____

Positive things that happened today:

_____

_____

_____

_____

How I felt today:

Happy	Inspired
Motivated	Optimistic
Creative	Excited
Focused	Hopeful
Reflective	

A goal for tomorrow:

Morning Meditation

Date: / /

todays focus:

_____

_____

_____

Affirmations for today:

_____

_____

_____

_____

Sleep I had last night:

Self-care to do today:

things I am grateful for today:

_____

_____

_____

_____

_____

Evening Reflection

Date: / /

Positive thoughts and feelings about today:

Positive things that happened today:

How I felt today:

Happy	Inspired
Motivated	Optimistic
Creative	Excited
Focused	Hopeful
Reflective	

A goal for tomorrow:

Morning Meditation

Date: / /

todays focus:

_____

_____

_____

Affirmations for today:

_____

_____

_____

_____

Sleep I had last night:

Self-care to do today:

things I am grateful for today:

_____

_____

_____

_____

_____

Evening Reflection

Date: / /

Positive thoughts and feelings about today:

_____
_____
_____
_____

Positive things that happened today:

_____
_____
_____
_____

How I felt today:

Happy	Inspired
Motivated	Optimistic
Creative	Excited
Focused	Hopeful
Reflective	

A goal for tomorrow:

Morning Meditation

Date: / /

todays focus:

_____

_____

_____

Affirmations for today:

_____

_____

_____

_____

Sleep I had last night:

Self-care to do today:

things I am grateful for today:

_____

_____

_____

_____

Evening Reflection

Date: / /

Positive thoughts and feelings about today:

Positive things that happened today:

How I felt today:

Happy	Inspired
Motivated	Optimistic
Creative	Excited
Focused	Hopeful
Reflective	

A goal for tomorrow:

"The only thing stopping you is you. Have complete faith in your dreams and watch them manifest before you."

-Soul Jotters

My achievements:

- .
- .
- .
- .
- .
- .
- .
- .
- .
- .
- .
- .
- .
- .
- .
- .
- .
- .

Printed in Great Britain
by Amazon